GREAT WARRIORS

MONGOLS

VALERIE BODDEN

CREATIVE EDUCATION • CREATIVE PAPERBACKS

Published by Creative Education and Creative Paperbacks
P.O. Box 227, Mankato, Minnesota 56002
Creative Education and Creative Paperbacks are imprints of The Creative Company
www.thecreativecompany.us

Design by Stephanie Blumenthal
Production by Christine Vanderbeek
Art direction by Rita Marshall
Printed in the United States of America and China

Photographs by Alamy (The Art Gallery Collection, North Wind Picture Archives, Photos 12, nik
wheeler), Corbis (The Gallery Collection), Getty Images (After Grigori Grigorevich Gagarin, Nelson Ching/
Bloomberg, Izabela Habur, Wolfgang Kaehler), iStockphoto (Dimedrol68, javarman3, Konstantin Kikvidze),
Shutterstock (Murat Besler, E. Karnejeff), SuperStock (DeAgostini, Exactostock, Pantheon, SuperStock)

Library of Congress Cataloging-in-Publication Data
Bodden, Valerie.
Mongols / Valerie Bodden.
p. cm. — (Great warriors)
Includes bibliographical references and index.
Summary: A simple introduction to the Central Asian warriors known as Mongols, including their history,
lifestyle, weapons, and how they remain a part of today's culture through their descendants.
ISBN 978-1-60818-468-2 (hardcover)
ISBN 978-1-62832-068-8 (pbk)
1. Mongols—Juvenile literature. I. Title.
DS19.B64 2013
950'.2—dc23   2012051837

PBK
2 4 6 8 9 7 5 3

TABLE OF CONTENTS

Sometimes people fight.

They fight for food. They fight for land.

Or sometimes they fight for sport.

Mongols were warriors who fought to

gain more land for their **empire**.

Mongols sometimes met in tents to talk about peace

The Mongol Empire was formed in Central Asia around 1000 A.D. Mongols fought other people in Asia and parts of Europe (*YOO-rup*).

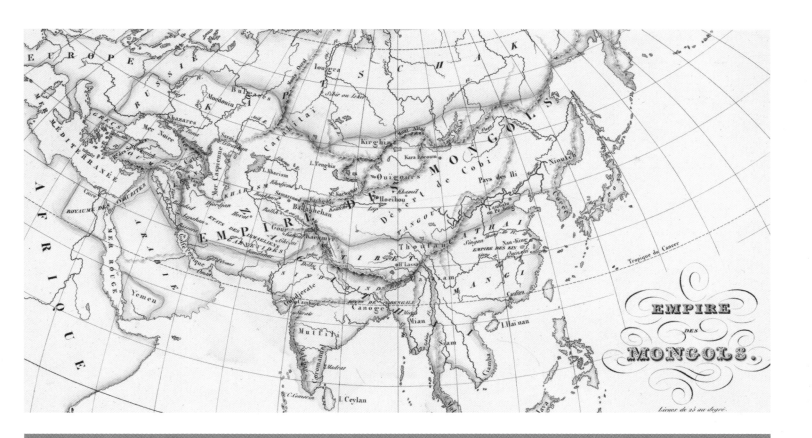

THE MONGOL EMPIRE WAS AT ITS LARGEST

AROUND THE YEAR 1300 A.D.

All Mongol men were warriors. Young boys were taught to care for and ride horses. They practiced making their horses run fast and stop suddenly. They learned to ride with no hands.

Mongolian warriors could use weapons while riding horseback

Most Mongol battles were fought on horseback. Many Mongol warriors used bows and arrows. They used axes and spears to fight, too.

MONGOLIAN HORSES ARE SHORTER THAN MANY OTHER HORSE BREEDS AND LIVE OUTDOORS YEAR-ROUND.

A Mongol warrior's most important tool was his horse. Mongols wore light-weight clothing that let them move around easily. They wore a silk shirt and leather **tunic**. Some wore leather helmets, too.

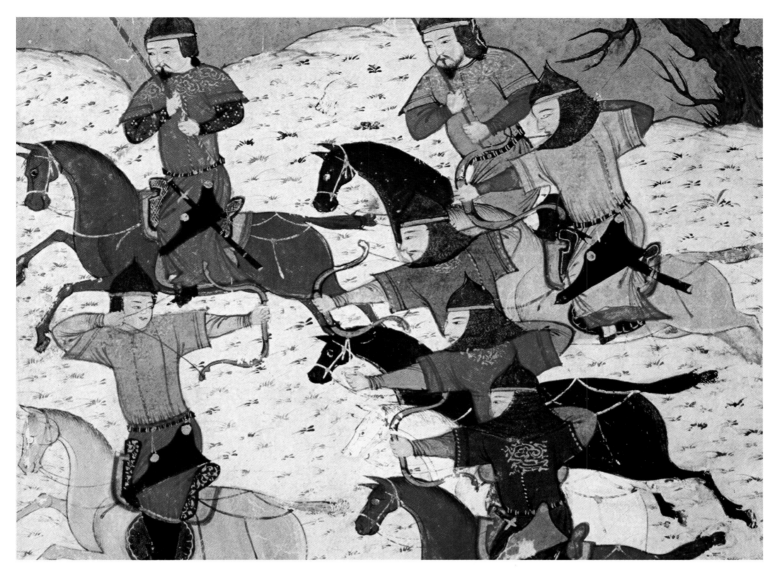

THE MONGOLS' SILK SHIRTS
DID NOT TEAR WHEN AN
ARROW WENT THROUGH.

Many people were scared of Mongols. Sometimes people **surrendered** before the Mongols attacked. Mongols liked playing tricks on their enemies. They pretended to run away. Then they turned around and fought! After a battle, the Mongols made the land they had taken part of their empire.

China built the Great Wall to keep out Mongols

A MONGOL WARRIOR'S WIFE BUILT
AND TOOK CARE OF THE FAMILY'S YURT.

At home, many Mongol warriors had families. A family lived in a yurt. This was a round tent made of wooden poles and animal skins. Mongols were nomadic. That means they moved from place to place a lot.

Genghis Khan was the most famous Mongol of all. He **united** the different Mongol groups. Around 1206 A.D., he became ruler of the Mongols. Genghis Khan's grandson Batu helped the Mongol Empire fight for land in eastern Europe.

Genghis Khan ruled the Mongols for about 20 years

By the late 1300s, the Mongol Empire could no longer control all its lands. Its leaders began to fight each other. Soon the empire came to an end. Today, Mongols live in the country of Mongolia. Mongol warriors live on in them and in their stories!

MONGOLIAN PEOPLE STILL KEEP HORSES, SHOOT ARROWS,
AND PICTURE GENGHIS KHAN ON MONEY.

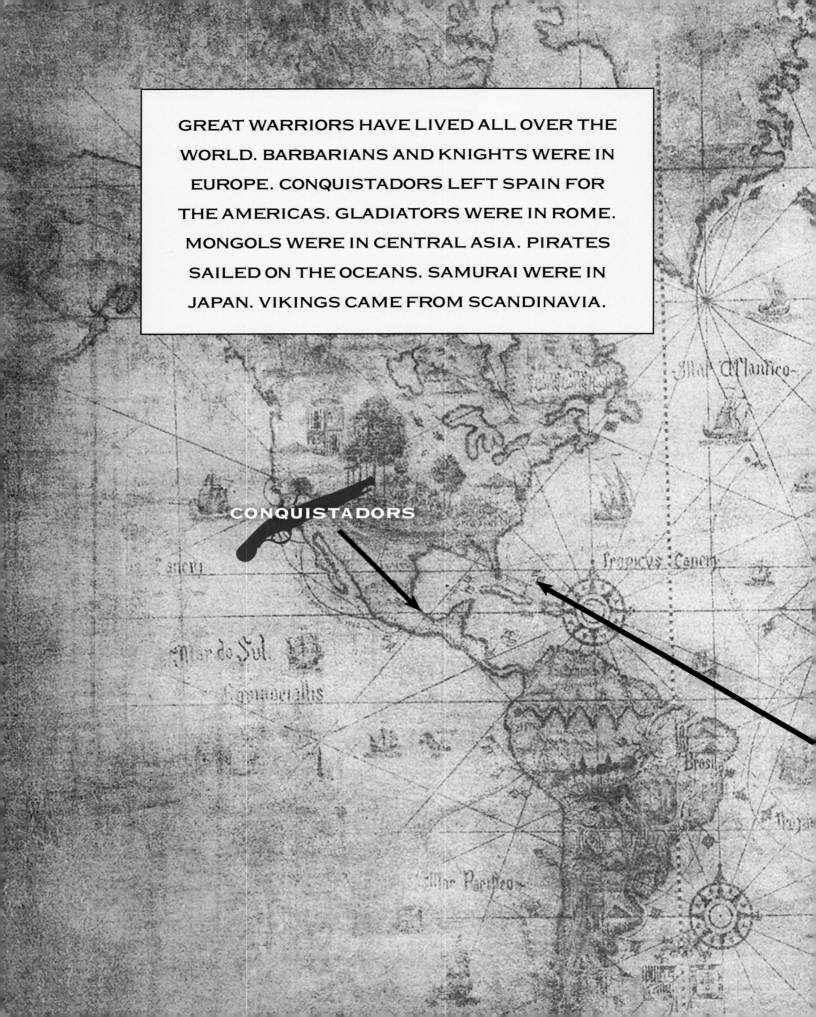

GREAT WARRIORS HAVE LIVED ALL OVER THE WORLD. BARBARIANS AND KNIGHTS WERE IN EUROPE. CONQUISTADORS LEFT SPAIN FOR THE AMERICAS. GLADIATORS WERE IN ROME. MONGOLS WERE IN CENTRAL ASIA. PIRATES SAILED ON THE OCEANS. SAMURAI WERE IN JAPAN. VIKINGS CAME FROM SCANDINAVIA.

CONQUISTADORS

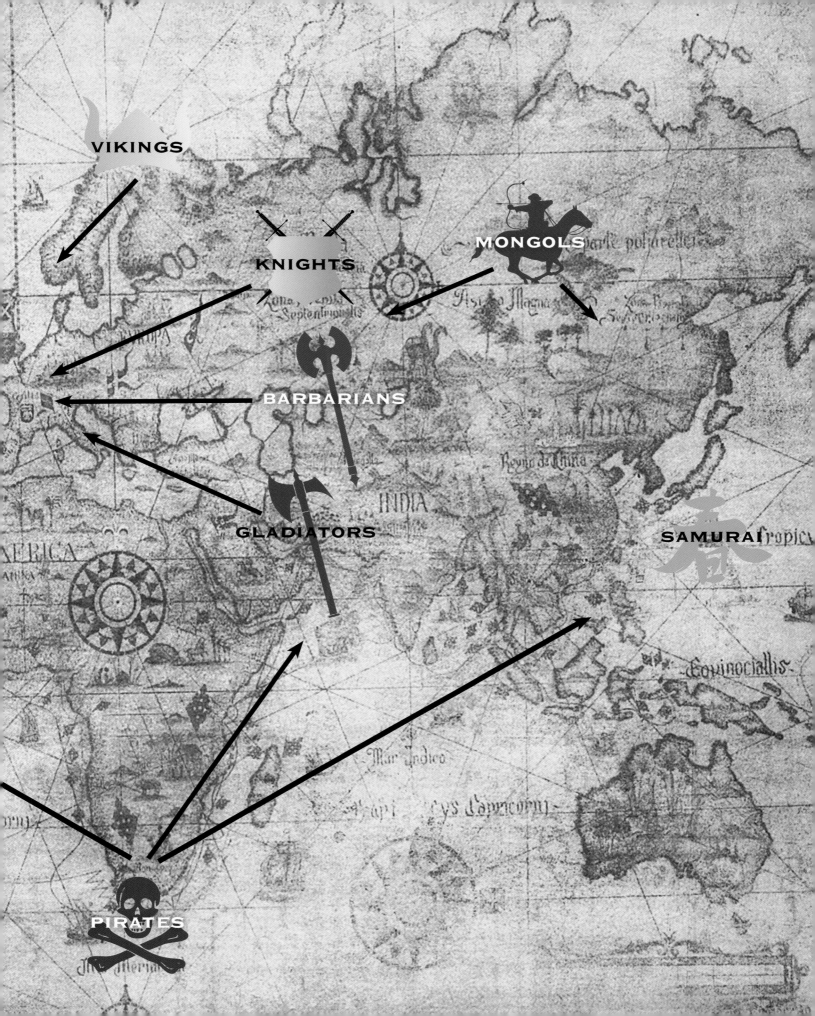

GLOSSARY

empire—many lands that are ruled by one leader

surrendered—gave up and said that the enemy won

tunic—a long, loose coat

united—joined together

READ MORE

Dittmar, Brian. *Mongol Warriors*. Minneapolis: Bellwether Media, 2012.

Pipe, Jim. *Wild Warriors*. North Mankato, Minn.: Smart Apple Media, 2011.

INDEX